APOLOGE

a course teaching Christians how to defend the Christian Faith

Instructor: Phil Fernandes, Ph.D.

Institute of Biblical Defense
P. O. Box 3264
Bremerton, WA. 98310
(360) 698-7382

THE BIBLICAL BASIS FOR APOLOGETICS

I) <u>What is Apologetics ?</u>
- A) <u>Definition</u> - the defense of the Christian Faith
- B) <u>Seven Types of Methodologies</u>
  - 1) philosophical
  - 2) historical
  - 3) scientific
  - 4) comparative religious
  - 5) presuppositional
  - 6) testimonial
  - 7) psychological

II) <u>Fideism</u>
- A) <u>Soren Kierkegaard (1813-1855)</u>
  - 1) Danish philosopher and theologian
  - 2) faith and reason do not meet
  - 3) subjective truth more important than objective truth
  - 4) blind leap of faith into the non-rational realm
  - 5) Christianity should not be defended, only believed
- B) <u>Traditional Apologists (Augustine, Aquinas, etc.)</u>
  - 1) Christianity is a reasonable faith
  - 2) our faith can be defended (1 Cor 15:14,17)

III) <u>The Biblical Basis for Apologetics</u>
- A) <u>The Bible commands it</u>
  - (1 Pt 3:15; Col 4:5-6; Titus 1:7-9; Jude 3)
- B) <u>The Bible speaks of natural revelation</u>
  - (Ps 14:1; 19:1; 94:9; Rm 1:18-22; 2:14-15; Heb 3:4)
- C) <u>The Bible speaks of historical evidences</u> (1 Cor 15:3-8)
- D) <u>The early church defended the faith</u>
  - 1) Peter (Acts 2:32; 3:15; 5:30-32; 10:39-41)
  - 2) John (Jn 20:30-31)
  - 3) Luke (Acts 1:1-3)
  - 4) Jude (Jude 3)
  - 5) Apollos (Acts 18:24, 28)
  - 6) Paul (Acts 9:22; 17:2-3, 31; 18:4; 19:8-10)

IV) Why is Apologetics Needed ?

A) To confirm the faith of believers

B) To persuade non-believers by removing intellectual stumbling blocks

C) To stand up for what is right even when no one is listening

D) To show the world Christianity is not irrational

THE FAILURE OF ATHEISTIC ARGUMENTS

I) Introduction
    A) <u>Atheism</u> - the belief that God definitely does not exist.
    B) <u>Agnosticism</u> - the belief that man cannot know if God exists.
    C) <u>Both are self-refuting</u>
        1) <u>atheism</u> - must be all-knowing to disprove God's
            existence
        2) <u>agnosticism</u> - must know something about God to
            know that nothing can be known
            about God.
        3) finite cannot reach infinite on its own
        4) still, infinite can reach finite (Mt 19:25-26)

II) God as a Product of Man's Imagination
    A) <u>Ludwig Feuerbach</u> - due to fear of death, man created God
        by his imagination. (God is what man wishes to be)
    B) <u>Sigmund Freud</u> - due to man's guilt for hating his father and
        man's fear of nature, man deifies nature and personal-
        izes it into a Father God.
    C) This explains false idols, but no one wishes for the God of
        the Bible.
    D) Not actually an argument against God's existence. Rather,
        it is an attempt by atheists to explain why so many
        people believe in a non-existent God.
    E) <u>Friedrich Nietzsche</u> - God is dead and traditional values have
        died with Him. Supermen must have the courage to
        create their own hard values rather than the soft values
        of Christianity (Hitler).

III) A.J. Ayer (Logical Positivism)
    A) God-talk is meaningless.
    B) verification principle - truth can only be found through the
        five senses.

C) verification principle itself cannot be proven through the
five senses.
D) words have the same meaning, but are applied finitely to
man, but infinitely to God. (analogical - similar;
equivocal - totally different; univocal - totally the same)

IV) Jean-Paul Sartre (French existentialist)
A) God is self-caused (response - God is uncaused)
B) Since man is free, God cannot exist (response - God
sovereignly chose to make man free)

V) Bertrand Russell (British philosopher)
A) if everything needs a cause, then so does God.
B) if God doesn't need a cause, neither does the universe.
C) response - only that which has a beginning needs a cause,
and the universe has a beginning.

VI) Argument from the Existence of Evil
A) an all-good God would want to destroy evil.
B) an all-powerful God is able to destroy evil.
C) but evil is not destroyed, it still exists.
D) therefore, no all-good and all-powerful God exists.
E) Christian response
1) unnecessary time limit on God (God is in the process
of defeating evil).
2) God created the possibility for evil (human free will),
not evil itself. (evil is a privation)
3) God allows evil for the purpose of a greater good
(human free will).
4) God's love cannot be forced on His creatures.
5) this is not the greatest possible world (this is the
greatest possible way to achieve the greatest possible
world - heaven).
6) man's free choice brought evil and human suffering
into the world.
7) God will use evil for good purposes (love enemies,
courage, etc., Isaiah 55:8-9).
8) atheists usually deny the existence of evil.
9) God will defeat evil through Christ's death, resurrection, and return.

10) the God of the Bible is the only guarantee that evil
will ultimately be defeated.

VII) Albert Camus (French existentialist, *The plague*)

A) man's dilemma - God allowed the plague, to fight the plague
is to fight God. To be religious, one must be antihuman-
itarian.

B) Christian response - God is fighting the plague of sin and its
effects, the godly man will fight it also.

VIII) Arguments from Contradictory Attributes

A) First Argument
1) an all-powerful God can do anything
2) even create a rock that He cannot lift
3) but if He can't lift this rock, He's not all-powerful
4) therefore, no all-powerful God exists

B) Response
1) God is all-powerful, but there are things even He
cannot do (fail, sin, lie, change mind)
2) God can't do what is impossible by nature (He can't
create square circles)
3) God will always be able to master His creation

C) Second Argument
1) either something is good because God wills it (good is
arbitrary)
2) or God wills it because it is good (good is above God)
3) therefore, either good is arbitrary or good is above
God

D) Response
1) God wills it because it is consistent with His own
good nature
2) the standard is not above God or arbitrary
3) God is the standard (God is good)

IX) Anthony Flew (British philosopher)

A) no way to falsify the invisible gardener
B) fails to admit the possibility of fulfilled prophecies, eye-
witnessed miracles, and the resurrection

X) The Absurdity of Life without God
      A) no meaning to life
      B) no objective morality
      C) no life after death (no rewards or punishments)
      D) no defeat of evil

XI) The Real Problem with Atheists
      A) not intellectual (not the mind)
      B) the problem is moral (the will)
      C) Rm 1:18-22; Jn 3:19-21
      D) man's two greatest drives
            1) transcendence (his thirst for God)
            2) autonomy (his desire to be his own god)

CREATION SCIENCE

I) Brief History of the Evolution-Creation Debate

A) Creation Model
1) dominated modern science before 1860
2) modern science started by men who believed in God's existence
3) Galileo, Isaac Newton, Francis Bacon, Johannes Kepler and Blaise Pascal
4) their belief in God's existence formed the basis for modern science
5) they believed that a reasonable God created the universe in a reasonable way, so that through reason man can find out about the universe in which we live
6) evolutionists have thrown out this base for modern science
7) without a reasonable God, can the universe really make sense?

B) Evolution Model
1) dominated modern science after 1860
2) 1860-Charles Darwin published "The Origin of Species"
3) he proposed a naturalistic explanation for the origin of the universe, first life, and new life forms
4) he taught that nature can be explained without appealing to a supernatural origin
5) this became the dominant view in science since 1860

II) The Scientific Method (evolution-not a scientific fact)
A) observation
B) proposal of a question or problem
C) hypothesis (educated guess)
D) experimentation
E) theory (a hypothesis with a high degree of probability)
F) natural law (a theory shown to be valid on a universal scale)

III) Evolution
     A) not a proven fact
     B) not a scientific law
     C) not a scientific theory (not repeatable, not open to observation and testing)
     D) only a scientific model (a way to interpret the evidence)

IV) Creation
     A) same category as evolution
     B) only a scientific model

V) Forensic Science (crime scene investigation)
     A) not operation science (repeatable, science of the present)
     B) origin science (Non-repeatable, science of the past, singular events)
          1) no direct observation is possible
          2) deals with singular, non-repeatable events of the past
          3) supposed evolutionary changes are non-repeatable
          4) supposed special creation is non-repeatable
          5) 2 principles are used instead of the scientific method
               a) uniformity or analogy (we posit the same kind of causes that we see making certain effects in the present for similar effects in the past)
               b) causality (every event has an adequate cause)
          6) which model (evolution or creation) is more plausible?
               a) both deal with the same evidence (common anatomy)
               b) both interpret the evidence differently
                    1) evolution (common ancestry)
                    2) creation (common Designer)

VI) Which Model is More Plausible?
     A) the origin of the universe
          1) energy deterioration (2nd Law of Thermodynamics)
               a) amount of usable energy in the universe is running down
               b) universe is winding down, it had to be wound up
               c) universe is going to end, it had to have a beginning

   d) the expansion of the universe confirms this

   e) the big bang model confirms this

2) creation model is more plausible

   a) the universe had a beginning

   b) something outside the universe had to cause it to exist

   c) the universe could not have evolved from nothing

   d) the universe is not eternal, it had a beginning

B) <u>the origin of first life</u>

   1) evolution-spontaneous generation (life came from non-life without intelligent intervention)

   2) creation-an Intelligent Being intervened to bridge the gap from non-life to life

   3) spontaneous generation violates the law of biogenesis and the cell theory

   4) natural laws by themselves do not produce specified complexity (highly complex information)

      a) natural laws can explain the Grand Canyon (Geisler)

      b) natural laws cannot explain the faces on Mount Rushmore (Geisler)

      c) a single-celled animal contains enough genetic information to fill an entire library

      d) explosion-print shop-dictionary

      e) intelligent intervention is needed to produce specified complexity

   5) creation model is more plausible

      a) Carl Sagan (single message from outer space would prove intelligent life on other planets, but a library of information got here by chance)

      b) Wickramasinghe (life couldn't be produced by non-intelligence)

C) <u>the origin of new life forms</u>

   1) fossil record

      a) new life forms appear suddenly and fully developed

      b) gaps in fossil record (no evidence for missing links)

2) human brain
- a) contains enough information to fill 20 million volumes of encyclopedia
- b) natural law cannot produce 20 million volumes of encyclopedia from one library's worth of information (a single-celled animal)
- c) again, intelligent intervention is needed to impart more complex information
- d) evolutionists point to mutations as the process by which evolution takes place
- e) however, mutations do not add more complex information to the genetic code
- f) mutations only garble the genetic code
- g) you can't go from the simple to the complex through natural law alone
- h) time plus chance plus natural laws never produce more complex information
- i) where did single-celled animals get genes for teeth?

3) creation model is more plausible

VII) Conclusion of our 3 Scientific Tests
- A) creationists have never seen the invisible Creator
- B) evolutionists have never seen the supposed evolutionary changes of the past
- C) the principles of uniformity and causality declare creationism to be a far superior model than that of evolution
- D) the universe needs a supernatural Cause
- E) this cause must be an intelligent Being to bring life from non-life and complex life forms from simple life forms

VIII) Major Problems With Evolution
- A) Energy Conservation (first law of thermodynamics)
  - 1) amount of energy in universe is constant
  - 2) no energy is now being created or destroyed
  - 3) whatever "process" brought the universe into existence is no longer in operation today

B) <u>Energy Deterioration (second law of thermodynamics)</u>
    1) amount of usable energy is running down
    2) universe will have an end, it had to have a beginning
    3) nature needs a supernatural cause
    4) Big Bang model and the expansion of the universe
       also confirm the beginning of the universe (from
       nothing, nothing comes)

C) <u>Evolutionary Dating Methods (inconsistent & unreliable)</u>
    1) based on uniformitarianism (assumes no world-wide
       catastrophes)
    2) assumes a constant rate of decay
    3) rocks known to have been only a few hundred years
       old have been dated to be hundreds of millions of
       years old
    4) Dr. Henry Morris-many different ways to date the
       earth's age, but evolutionists only use those methods
      which give astronomically old dates since evolution
      needs millions of years to seem slightly possible
    5) some methods point to a very young earth (pop-
       ulation statistics, moon dust, earth's magnetic field)
    6) even an old earth doesn't refute creation model

D) <u>Fossil Record</u>
    1) assumed to prove evolution
    2) shows no evidence of missing links
    3) new life forms appear suddenly and fully developed
       (no half-fins or half-wings)
    4) could point to a world-wide flood
    5) fossilization is extremely rare today
    6) fossils caused by rapid burial (what a world-wide
       flood would do)
    7) canopy theory (Gen 1:6-8, 6:11-12; Ps 104:5-9)
    8) if earth were a smooth sphere, it would be covered
       with water 2 miles in depth
    9) flood would tend to bury fossils in this order:
        a) deep ocean creatures
        b) creatures in shallower water
        c) amphibians and land-bordering creatures
        d) swamp, marsh, and low river-flat creatures
          (especially reptiles)

        e) higher mammals who retreated to higher
           ground attempting to escape the flood
        f) last, humans would be overtaken
    10) exceptions explained by upheavals in earth's crust
       after flood
    11) global ice age would follow flood
    12) lack of vegetation will kill off dinosaurs (Job,
       Japanese fishermen, African natives, legends)

E) <u>Mutations</u>
    1) don't prove evolution
    2) evolution needs new genes
    3) only alter already existing genes
    4) where did single-celled animals get genes for teeth?

F) <u>Supposed Missing Links Between Apes and Men</u>
    1) Neanderthal Man (features of modern man)
    2) Cro-Magnon Man (features of modern man)
    3) Colorado Man (member of the horse family)
    4) Java Man (Pithecanthropus-a large gibbon)
    5) Heidelberg Man (only consisted of a lower jaw)
    6) Piltdown Man (a clever hoax)
    7) Peking Man (a large monkey or baboon)
    8) Southern Ape (Australopithecus-an extinct ape)
    9) Rama Pithecus (an extinct ape)
    10) East African Man (Zinjanthropus-an ape)
    11) Dryopithecus (an extinct ape)
    12) Nebraska Man (1925 trial-tooth of an extinct pig)

G) <u>Archaeopteryx (thought to be transitionary form between reptiles and birds)</u>
    1) teeth, lizard-like tail, claws like a reptile
    2) wings and feathers like a bird
    3) fully-developed (now classified as a bird)

H) <u>Punctuated Equilibrium (Steven Gould)</u>
    1) 130 years since Darwin, still no missing links
    2) Punctuated Equilibrium-there are none
    3) 2 apes had a baby boy?
    4) evolution means gradual change
    5) Punctuated Equilibrium-sudden changes
    6) has evolution been abandoned?
    7) Punctuated Equilibrium attempts to explain away the
       lack of evidence for evolution

I) <u>Heisenberg's Principle of Indeterminacy</u>
    1) a theory in quantum physics
    2) subatomic particle movement is presently unpredictable for man
    3) does not mean things happen without a cause
    4) simply means that scientists aren't yet able to accurately predict where a specific particle will be at a given time
    5) Max Planc (Physicist who holds above view)
    6) man is limited in knowledge
    7) if things can occur without a cause, science crumbles

J) <u>Many Unproven Assumptions</u>
    1) <u>no evidence for spontaneous generation</u>
        a) violates cell theory & law of biogenesis
        b) <u>Miller and Urey experiments</u>
            1) attempt to bring life from non-life in lab
            2) if successful-only shows intelligent intervention is needed
            3) Geisler-production of amino acids is as far from producing life as a single sentence is from one volume of an encyclopedia (or an entire library)
            4) Wickramasinghe-calls these experiments cheating
    2) <u>universe not eternal</u>
    3) <u>universe couldn't evolve from nothing</u>
    4) <u>no proof for:</u>
        a) intelligence coming from non-intelligence
        b) multi-celled animals coming from single-celled animals (embryo doesn't evolve into a human, full genetic code is in place at conception)
        c) animals with backbones coming from animals without backbones
        d) no evidence for common ancestry of fish, reptiles, birds, and mammals (common anatomy points to common design)
    5) <u>evolution itself is an unproven assumption</u>

IX) Closing Remarks

    A) <u>Evolution needs God</u>

    B) <u>God doesn't need evolution</u>

    C) If evolution is true, God is still needed to bring the universe into existence from nothing, to bring life from non-life, and complex life forms from simple life forms. For, in each case, a miraculous superseding of natural laws is needed.

    D) But, if God exists, He doesn't need evolution. He could have merely started the long evolutionary process or He could have created the universe in 6 days.

    E) God could have used evolution, but if He did, He left absolutely no evidence. He would have covered His tracks. But would this not make God the author of deception?

    F) Once Galileo was scoffed at by fellow scientists for believing the earth revolved around the sun. Now creationists are being ridiculed for saying, "in the beginning, God created the heavens and the earth."

    G) As the decades pass, creation science will be vindicated just as Galileo was vindicated by future study.

    H) Unfortunately, many evolutionists may never be able to abandon the blind faith they hold in the dead and unscientific religion called "evolution."

EVIDENCE FOR GOD'S EXISTENCE

I) Arguments for God's Existence
    A) <u>Cosmological</u>-cause and effect, universe needs a cause
        (Ps 19:1; Rm 1:18-22; Heb 3:4)
    B) <u>Teleological</u>-universe is a product of intelligent design
        (Ps 94:9)
    C) <u>Moral</u>-universal moral law implies a universal law Giver
        (Rm 2:14-15)
    D) <u>Religious Experience</u>-all men sense a need for God (Mt 4:4)
    E) <u>Ontological Argument</u>-idea of God-a being who cannot not
        exist

II) Thomas Aquinas (1224-1274 AD) Cosmological-existential causality
    A) beings exist which are dependent on other beings for their continuing existence
    B) dependent beings cannot be the ultimate cause of the continuing existence of other dependent beings
    C) adding dependent beings never gives us an independent being
    D) the ultimate cause for the continuing existence of all dependent beings must be an independent Being
    E) modern proponent-Geisler

III) Leibniz (1646-1716) Cosmological-sufficient reason
    A) there is a sufficient reason for everything that exists
    B) the existence of some beings is explained by something other than itself (parents, air, food, water, etc.)
    C) the collection of all these beings needs an explanation
    D) an infinite regress of sufficient reasons is impossible (then there would be no explanation at all)
    E) therefore, there must exist a Being who contains within itself the reason for its own existence (this Being explains the existence of itself and all other beings)
    F) modern proponent-Copleston

IV) Bonaventure (1221-1274) Cosmological-Kalam
A) whatever had a beginning needs a cause
B) the universe had a beginning
C) the universe needs a cause
D) an infinite regress is impossible
E) the cause of the universe must be eternal
F) modern proponent-Craig

V) William Paley (1743-1805 AD) Teleological
A) a watch, because of its design, implies a watchmaker
B) the universe is one of design (life on earth, single-cell)
C) the universe is the product on an intelligent Designer
D) print shop-explosions-Webster's Dictionary

VI) C. S. Lewis (1898-1963) moral
A) all admit to an objective moral standard (when we are wronged)
B) nature is non-moral
C) the objective moral standard must come from a supernatural Cause (reason also)

VII) Francis Schaeffer (1912-1984)
A) only 3 possible explanations:
   1) everything came from nothing
   2) everything had an impersonal start
   3) everything had a personal start
B) from nothing, nothing comes
C) personal man could not come from an impersonal cause
D) therefore, everything had a personal start

VIII) Phil Fernandes (1960-not real soon) this argument builds upon the work of the philosophers mentioned above

A) Some dependent beings now exist
   1) I must exist in order to deny my existence (actual undeniability-Geisler)
   2) when I communicate with others, I affirm their existence
   3) I am dependent on many things for my continued existence (air, water, food, etc.)

4) others live like dependent beings (the denial of dependency is forced and temporary-principle used by Hodge)

5) the denial of the physical world is forced and temporary

B) <u>From nothing, nothing comes</u>

1) nothing is nothing, therefore nothing does nothing

2) therefore, nothing can cause nothing

C) <u>Something must be eternal</u>

1) if there was ever nothing existing, then there would be nothing now (for from nothing, nothing comes)

2) but, some dependent beings now exist

3) therefore, something must be eternal (no beginning or end)

D) <u>This eternal something cannot be the universe</u>

1) an eternal universe would mean an actual infinite set of finite events

2) an actual infinite set of finites existing outside the mind is impossible

    a) Set A = (1, 2, 3, 4, 5, 6, . . .)

    b) Set B = (1, 3, 5, 7, 9, . . .)

    c) Set C = (10, 20, 30, 40, 50, . . .)

3) all three sets are equal (they are all infinite)

4) all three sets are not equal

    a) Set A is twice as large as Set B

    b) Set A is ten times as large as Set C

5) any view that generates contradictions and absurdities is false

6) if the universe is eternal, we could never reach *now*

    a) it is impossible to traverse an infinite set of finite events

    b) Zeno's Paradox - impossible to traverse an actual infinite set of finite points

E) <u>This eternal something must be the uncaused Cause of everything else that exists</u>

1) for from nothing, nothing comes

2) dependent beings are caused by the eternal Something

F) <u>There is intelligent and moral life in the universe</u>

1) without intelligence, there could be no thought or communication

2) without morality, there could be no such thing as right and wrong

G) <u>Intelligence and morality cannot come from nature (nature is non-intelligent and non-moral)</u>

H) <u>The eternal uncaused Cause of everything else that exists must be an intelligent and moral Being (a personal Being)</u>

I) <u>As the source of all else that exists, this eternal uncaused Cause must be unlimited in all His attributes</u>
  1) <u>all-powerful</u> (He is the source of all power in the universe, no other power can limit Him)
  2) <u>all-knowing</u> (He is the source of all knowledge)
  3) <u>sovereign</u> (as Creator, He cannot be mastered by His creation)
  4) <u>all-good</u> (He is the source of all the good in the universe, He is not limited by evil)
  5) <u>perfect</u> (He is the standard by which all else is measured)
  6) <u>immaterial</u> (not limited by matter)
  7) <u>every-where present</u> (not limited by space)
  8) <u>eternal</u> (not limited by time)
  9) <u>one</u> (2 infinite beings would limit one another, but this is impossible since to be infinite means to be unlimited by any other being. Also, for 2 beings to differ, one being must have something that the other one lacks. But if one being lacks some perfection, then he cannot be infinite. Only one being can be infinite.)

J) <u>As the source of all finite existence, the eternal uncaused Cause must be immanent (involved with) and transcendent (separate from) in relation to His creation.</u>
  1) <u>immanent</u> (he sustains all finite existence, for what cannot cause its own existence, can't keep itself in existence)
  2) <u>transcendent</u> (He is infinite, His creation is finite. He is not identical to the universe)

OLD TESTAMENT RELIABILITY

I) Old Testament Manuscripts
  A) Hebrew
    1) Dead Sea Scrolls (150-100BC)
    2) Masoretic Text (1010AD) entire Old Testament,
       standard text today
  B) Greek - Septuagint (250-150BC) translation of Hebrew O.T.

II) Definitions
  A) lower criticism - restoring original text on the basis of
     imperfect copies (textual criticism)
  B) higher criticism - authorship, date, & integrity of each book
  C) form criticism - seeks to find the supposed oral traditions
     that lie behind the written documents (extremely
     subjective)
  D) documentary hypothesis - theory that the Pentateuch was a
     compilation of different written documents composed by
     different authors at different places and different times
     long after Moses
  E) common liberal bias - atheistic evolution
    1) revelation, prophecy, & miracles are impossible
    2) polytheism evolved into monotheism

III) Documentary Hypothesis (Its History)
  A) Jean Astruc - different divine names point to different
     sources (Elohim & Jehovah) 1753
  B) Wilhelm M. L. DeWette - Deuteronomy was written at the
     start of Josiah's reformation to unify worship of the Jews in
     621BC (1806)
  C) Hermann Hupfeld - divided Elohim document into E1 and
     E2, one part later became Priestly Code (1853)
  D) Abraham Kuener - gave the JEDP order (1869)
  E) Julius Wellhausen - supported JEDP with evolutionary view
     of religion (animism evolved into polytheism, which
     evolved into monalatry, which evolved into monotheism)
     1878

F) <u>Final Conclusion</u>
    1) Jehovah (850BC)
    2) Elohim (750BC)
    3) Deuteronomy (621BC)
    4) Priestly Code (570-530BC)

IV) <u>Refutation of Documentary Hypothesis</u>

A) 20th century scholarship repudiates this view, still turns to more liberal speculation
B) circular reasoning (assumes revelation is impossible to prove Bible is a human book)
C) explain away opposing evidence with hypothetical editor
D) teach that only Hebrews couldn't use more than one name for God (Babylon, Ugarit, Egypt, Greece, Islam)
E) assume secular history is always right when it differs with Biblical account
F) assumes Hebrew religion evolved into monotheism (Israel was only nation to have a true monotheistic faith)
G) take passages out of context to prove the Bible has contradictions, no solution is accepted
H) reject evidence for much semetic repetition in literature by same author
I) assume they can scientifically reconstruct the text 3,000 years later

V) <u>Evidences for Mosaic Authorship of Pentateuch</u> <u>(1450-1410BC)</u>

A) the unity of the first five books
B) Pentateuch, Old & New Testaments, Jesus call Moses the author (Josh 8:31; 1 Kn 2:3; Dn 9:11; Mk 12:26; Lk 20:28; Rm 10:5)
C) eyewitness details in the Pentateuch
D) author - acquainted with Egypt, unfamiliar with Canaan
E) desert atmosphere and point of view
F) 2nd millennium BC customs
G) greater percentage of Egyptian words than rest of Bible
H) Moses' qualifications (education, knowledge of Egypt & Sinai) Acts 7:22
I) different divine names used for different contexts
    1) Elohim (creation & power)
    2) Jehovah (covenant relationship)

J) variation in diction and style
>> 1) different types of literature (genealogies, biographies, historical accounts)
>> 2) author varied text to prevent monotony
>> 3) parrallel accounts were poetic style

K) Biblical evidence shows Jewish faith was originally monotheistic, Jews later became idolatrous

L) study of ancient religions show that primitive peoples had technical sacrificial language

M) writing existed during Moses' time (1500BC-Ras Shamra literature)

N) archaeological finds confirm pentateuch (city of Ur, Schechem & Bethel, Hittite Legal Code, use of camels)

O) Code Of Hammurabi - 1800BC (similar to Mosaic Laws)

P) Numbers - similar to 1800BC Mari texts census lists

Q) Deuteronomy - same format as Hittite suzerainty treaty (latter half of 2nd millennium, between king & his people)

R) ancient legends of creation and worldwide flood throughout world (possible perversions of the true Biblical accounts)

S) Jews accepted the Law as Mosaic during Josiah's reform in 621BC, hard to believe any large portion had just been written

VI) Joshua & the Conquest of the Promised Land
A) Amarna Tablets (1400-1350BC)
B) reports from kings in Palestine area to Egypt requesting assistance against Hapiru invaders

VII) Isaiah (740-680BC)
A) Deutero-Isaiah theory (2 authors; 1-39, 40-66)
B) attempts to explain away fulfilled prophecies
C) Refutation
>> 1) author is familiar with Palestine, not Babylon
>> 2) predictions of the Medo-Persian overthrow of Babylon in first section (13:17-19) 538BC
>> 3) similar style in both halves of Isaiah
>> 4) Jn 12:37-41 (Isa 53 and Isa 6 quoted)

VIII) The Book Of Daniel
A) Liberal View
>> 1) written about 165BC
>> 2) to encourage resistance to Antiochus Epiphanes

3) critics refuse to accept predictive prophecy

4) attempt to date Daniel after events already occurred

B) Conservative View

    1) book completed by 530BC

    2) Daniel lived during both the Babylonian and the Medo-Persian rule over Judah

C) The Evidence

    1) archaeological confirmation of historical characters

        a) King Belshazzar (cuneiform tablets)

        b) Darius the Mede (Gubaru, Darius - title like Caesar)

    2) 3 Greek words in Daniel (musical instruments, Greeks took over Palestine in 330BC)

    3) Daniel uses early Aramaic

    4) Daniel's theology does not prove a late date (angels, resurrection, Kingdom of God)

    5) some of Daniel's predictions fulfilled after 165BC

D) Prediction of the 4 Kingdoms (Dan 2, 7)

    1) Babylon (586BC - took Judah captive)

    2) Medo-Persian 538BC (3 ribs in mouth-Babylon, Egypt, Lydia)

    3) Greece 330BC (4 way split)

    4) Rome 63BC (2 legs, 10 toes)

E) Messianic Prophecies (Dan 9:24-27)

    1) Messiah executed (30-33AD)

    2) temple destroyed (70AD)

F) Conclusion

    1) evidence supports 530BC date of Daniel

    2) even 165BC date would have to admit major fulfillments of prophecies

    3) no reason to doubt 530BC date

Reliability of the New Testament Manuscripts

<u>Reference Works:</u>   Josephus, Apostolic Fathers, Fernandes (Diss.)
Habermas, <u>Ancient Evidence</u>

1) <u>Manuscript Evidence</u>
    A) N.T. - over 26,000 extant copies
        (Plato - 7, Homer's Iliad - 643)
    B) N.T. - earliest copy 25-35 years after original (John Rylands)
        (Plato - 1,200 years, Homer's Iliad - 500 years)
    C) N.T. - 99.5% accuracy, no contradictions in doctrine
        (Plato - ?, Homer's Iliad - 95%)
    D) <u>Famous New Testament Manuscripts</u>
        1) Dead Sea Scrolls fragment of Mark's Gospel? (50-70AD)
        2) John Ryland's Papyri (125-130AD) fragment - John 18
        3) Bodmer Papyrus II (150-200AD) most of John's Gospel
        4) Chester Beatty Papyri (200AD) major portions of N.T.
        5) Codex Vaticanus (325-350AD) almost entire Bible
        6) Codex Sinaiticus (350AD) almost all N.T., half of O.T.
        7) Codex Alexandrinus (400AD) almost entire Bible
        8) Codex Ephraemi (400's AD) almost every N.T. book
    E) <u>N. T. Manuscripts</u> - most reliable of all ancient writings

2) <u>Apostolic Fathers</u> (quoted N.T., taught Christ's deity, sacrificial
death, resurrection, and salvation only through Him)
    A) <u>Clement of Rome</u> (letter to Corinthians, 95AD) A.F. 67-68
    B) <u>Ignatius</u> (wrote 110-115AD) A.F. 137, 139, 144, 148-150
    C) <u>Polycarp</u> (lived 70-156AD, John's pupil) A.F. 177, 181
    D) <u>Papias</u> (lived 60-140AD) A.F. 528

3) <u>Ancient Secular Writings</u> (confirmed message of early church)
    A) <u>Thallus</u> (52AD) tried to explain away darkness at crucifixion
    B) <u>Cornelius Tacitus</u> (115AD) Roman historian, Habermas 87-88
    C) <u>Suetonius</u> (wrote 117-138AD) Roman historian, Hab. 89-90
    D) <u>Pliny the Younger</u> (wrote 112AD) Roman govenor, Hab. 95
    E) <u>Emperor Trajan</u> (112AD) deny Christ/set free, Hab. 96
    F) <u>Emperor Hadrian</u> (wrote 117-138AD) need proof/execution
    G) <u>Jewish Talmud</u> (70-200AD) Jesus/a sorcerer, Hab. 98
    H) <u>Lucian</u> (2nd century) Greek writer, Hab. 100
    I) <u>Josephus</u> (37-97AD) Jewish historian, Jos. 480, Hab. 91-92

4) <u>Ancient Creeds in the New Testament</u>
    A) predate the New Testament
    B) read more smooth in Aramaic (early church was Jewish)
    C) poetic style (creeds or hymns of early church)
    D) even critics date Paul's writings in 50's and 60's AD
    E) three examples of ancient creeds found in Paul's writings
        1) Romans 10:9 (Christ's deity & resurrection)
        2) 1 Corinthians 15:3-8 (Christ's resurrection)
        3) Philippians 2:6-11 (Christ's deity)

5) <u>New Testament Reliability confirmed by the Experts</u>
    A) A. T. Robertson
    B) Sir William Ramsey
    C) William F. Albright
    D) Sir Frederick Kenyon
    E) Millar Burrows
    F) F. F. Bruce
    G) Bruce Metzger

6) <u>Additional Evidences</u>
    A) <u>Matthew</u> testimony of Papias, originally written in Hebrew, tax collector - stenographer?, quoted very early
    B) <u>Mark</u> testimony of Papias, Peter's Gospel, quoted early
    C) <u>Luke & Acts</u> Acts was Luke's sequel, both addressed to Theophilus, Paul's death not recorded, quoted early
    D) <u>John</u> quoted or paraphrased by Ignatius, Polycarp & Papias
    E) <u>Paul's Letters</u> (except general epistles) widely accepted
    F) <u>Hebrews</u> before 70AD, temple sacrifices still offered

Did Jesus Rise?
Evidence for the Resurrection

1) Are Miracles Possible?
    A) David Hume's View (1711-1776) (stronger interpretation)
        1) miracles are violations of the laws of nature
        2) the laws of nature cannot be violated
        3) therefore, miracles cannot occur
    B) Refutation
        1) laws of nature are descriptive, not prescriptive
        2) laws of nature = regular processes God set in motion
        3) miracles = when God supersedes regular processes
    C) If God exists, miracles are possible
    D) Each miracle claim should be investigated, not ruled out
        beforehand due to philosophical assumptions

2) Christ's Resurrection Was Bodily
    A) Jehovah's Witnesses say Christ rose spiritually
    B) Mt 28:6; Jn 2:19, 21; 20:26-27; Lk 24:36-43; 1 Cor 15:42-44
    C) spiritual body = same body in glorified state

3) Importance of the Resurrection (1 Cor 15:14, 17; Rm 10:9)

4) Only Four Possibilities (legends, lies, apostles deceived, truth)

5) Resurrection Accounts Were Not Legends (prior lectures)
    A) Legends take centuries to form (long after eyewitnesses die)
    B) creeds found in New Testament date back to less than 20
        years after Christ's death (1 Cor 15:3-8; Rm 10:9)
    C) Apostolic Fathers (95-150AD) taught the resurrection
    D) New Testament manuscript evidence
    E) confirmed by ancient secular writings
    F) New Testament-most reliable ancient writing

6) Apostles Were Not Lying
    A) did not steal the body & fabricate the resurrection accounts
    B) claimed they saw resurrected Christ on numerous occassions

C) died martyrs' deaths refusing to deny resurrection

D) men do not die for what they know to be a hoax

E) therefore, the apostles sincerely believed they had seen the resurrected Christ on several occassions

7) Apostles Were Not Deceived

A) liberal scholars attempted to explain away the resurrection

1) swoon theory-Jn 19:31-34, side pierced/blood & water

2) wrong tomb theory (doesn't explain appearances, Jews would have found body)

3) hallucination theory (no 2 people have the same one)

B) the liberal scholars have themselves proven their own theories false

8) Apostles Were Telling the Truth

A) Resurrection accounts were not legends

B) Apostles were not lying

C) Apostles were not deceived

D) Conclusion: the apostles were telling the truth

9) Further Support For the Resurrection

A) Apostles changed the Sabbath to Sunday (devout Jews)

B) First century Jews were silent (no written refutation)

C) Church grew rapidly as the resurrection was proclaimed in Jerusalem (near the tomb)

D) the conversions of Paul and James

Is Jesus God?
Evidence for the Deity of Christ

Reference Works: The Center of Christianity, John Hick (27-28)
                            Mere Christianity, C. S. Lewis (56)

1) Jesus Claimed to be God
      A) John 5:17-18, 22-23; 8:23-24, 58-59; 10:28-33; 14:9; 17:5
      B) He accepted worship (Mt 14:33; 28:9; Jn 9:35-38; 20:26-29)
      C) He was arrested for blasphemy (Jn 10:33; Mk 14:64)
      D) the New Testament is historically reliable (not legend)
          1) written by sincere eyewitnesses (martyrs)
          2) authors stated that Christ claimed to be God

2) The Apostles Called Jesus God
      A) John (John 1:1, 14; 1 John 5:20)
      B) Matthew (Matthew 1:20-23)
      C) Peter (2 Peter 1:1)
      D) Thomas (John 20:26-29)
      E) Paul (Rm 9:5; Php 2:5-8; Col 2:9; Titus 2:13; Acts 20:28)

3) The Apostolic Fathers Called Jesus God (Polycarp, Ignatius)

4) Ancient Secular Authors Wrote that First-Century Christians Worshipped Jesus as God
      A) Pliny the Younger (wrote 112AD)
      B) Lucian (2nd Century, "Christians. . . worship a man to this
          day.")

5) Ancient Creeds Call Jesus God (Php 2:5-11; Rm 10:9; 1 Tm 3:16)

6) Our Choices:
      A) the deity of Christ is not a legend
      B) Jesus was not merely a good man (He claimed to be God)
      C) Jesus was either a liar, insane, or God

7) Jesus was not a Liar
      A) most recognize that Jesus taught the highest standards of
          morality ever taught

B) Jesus has had a positive impact on mankind like no other
man
C) Jesus' love and compassion for His fellow man does not fit
the profile of a selfish liar
D) Jesus' resurrection was genuine (would God raise a liar?)

8) <u>Jesus was not Insane</u>
A) Christ was the greatest teacher of all time (insane people
make lousy teachers)
B) Christ's miraculous life proves He wasn't insane
(Talmud/sorcery)
C) Christ's resurrection proves He wasn't insane
D) Christ's life and works were prophesied hundreds of years
before His birth
1) seed of Abraham (Gn 12:1-3)
2) tribe of Judah (Gn 49:10)
3) line of Jesse (Isa 11:1)
4) line of David (Jer 23:5)
5) virgin birth (Isa 7:14)
6) born in Bethlehem (Micah 5:2)
7) His forerunner (Isa 40:3)
8) executed before 70AD (Dn 9:24-27)
9) His miracles (Isa 35:4-6)
10) His parables (Ps 78:2)
11) rejected by the Jews (Isa 53; 65:1-2; 8:13-15)
12) wide Gentile following (Isa 42:1-4; 65:1-2)
13) betrayed for 30 pieces of silver (Zech 11:12-13)
14) forsaken by disciples (Zech 13:7)
15) enterred Jerusalem on donkey, received a king's
welcome (Zech 9:9)
16) silent before accusers (Isa 53:7)
17) crucified (Ps 22:16)
18) lots cast for His garments (Ps 22:18)
19) bones not broken (Ps 34:20; Ex 12:43-46)
20) side pierced (Zech 12:10)
21) buried in rich man's tomb (Isa 53:9)
22) resurrection (Ps 16:10)
23) ascension (Ps 68:18)
24) at the Father's right hand (Ps 110:1)
E) chances of Christ fulfilling just 16 prophecies by coincidence
are 1 in 10^{45} (a one with 45 zeros after it)

F) unlikely that an insane man's life would be prophesied hundreds of years before his birth (Greek Septuagint-200BC)

G) prophecies #8, 11, & 12 are enough to prove that Jesus is the Jewish Messiah

9) Conclusion-Jesus is God

A) Christ's deity was not a legend (eyewitness testimony)

B) Jesus was not merely a good man (He claimed to be God)

C) Jesus was not a liar(doesn't fit profile, miracles/resurrection)

D) Jesus was not insane (doesn't fit profile, miracles, resurrection)

E) therefore, Jesus is God (He proved Himself to be God by fulfilling prophecies, performing miracles, and rising from the dead)

Is The Bible God's Word?
Evidence For The Bible

1) <u>Things Already Proven in this Course</u>
    A) the existence of a personal, infinite God
    B) the historical reliability of the Old and New Testaments
    C) Jesus' bodily resurrection
    D) Christ's Deity

2) <u>Christ's Teaching About The Old Testament</u>
    A) Mt 5:17-18; 15:3-4; 22:31-32; Mk 7:9-13; Lk 11:49-51
    B) Jesus considered Old Testament the inerrant Word of God

3) <u>Christ's View of the New Testament</u>
    A) Mk 13:31; Jn 14:26; 15:26-27; 16:13; Acts 1:8
    B) Christ promised His teachings would be preserved
    C) the Holy Spirit would remind apostles of Christ's words
    D) the Holy Spirit would show the apostles future things
    E) the Holy Spirit would guide the apostles into the truth
    F) the Holy Spirit would empower the apostles to be Christ's
        representatives to the world
    G) conclusion: Christ promised to preserve His teachings
        through the apostle's writings
    H) Jesus is God and He declared the Bible (both Old and New
        Testaments) to be the inerrant Word of God

4) <u>Further Confirmation that the Bible is God's Word</u>
    A) Bible's supernatural wisdom
    B) fulfilled prophecies

5) <u>Bible's Supernatural Wisdom</u>
    A) only the Bible explains man's greatness & wretchedness
    B) only the Bible solves the problem of evil
    C) Bible's wisdom most cherished (#1 all-time best seller)
    D) 700BC-taught earth was a sphere (Isa 40:22)
    E) 2000BC-taught earth was suspended in space (Job 26:7)
    F) taught first & second laws of thermodynamics (Gen 2:1-3;
        Mk 13:31) not scientifically established until 1850AD

6) <u>Fulfilled Prophecies</u>
>	A) Tyre (Ezk 26:4, 5, 14) destroyed, barren, fishing nets
>	B) Sidon (Ezk 26:23) suffer violence, yet remain in existence
>	C) Ashkelon (Zeph 2:4) destroyed
>	D) Philistia (Zeph 2:5) extinct
>	E) Edomites (Obadiah 18) descendants of Esau/no survivors
>	F) Egypt (Isa 19:21, 22) still a nation in the last days
>	G) Israel (Hosea 9:17) scattered among the nations
>	H) Israel (Ezk 37:21; Isa 11:11-12) regathered in the last days
>	I) Israel (Gen 12:1-3) those who cursed her would be cursed
>>		-Egypt, Babylon, Assyria, Edom, Philistia, Rome,
>>			Nazi Germany
>	J) many other prophecies that have been fulfilled
>>		1) Jesus (last lecture)
>>		2) empires (Dan 2, 7)

7) <u>Summary of Evidence that Bible is God's Word</u>
>	A) Jesus, who is God, taught that the Bible is God's Word
>	B) the supernatural wisdom of the Bible
>	C) the fulfilled prophecies of the Bible

8) <u>Implications of the Bible being God's Word</u>
>	A) whatever it teaches is true
>>		1) its salvation message is true
>>>			a) man is a sinner & can't save himself
>>>				(Rm 3:10, 23; Mt 19:25-26)
>>>			b) Jesus took our punishment for us
>>>				(Jn 1:29; 2 Cor 5:15; 1 Pt 2:24; 3:18)
>>>			c) salvation comes only through Jesus
>>>				(Jn 14:6; Acts 4:12; Rm 6:23)
>>>			d) we must trust in Jesus to be saved
>>>				(Jn 3:16-18; Eph 2:8-9)
>>		2) its doctrines are true
>>>			a) the Trinity,
>>>			b) virgin birth, substitutionary death, & 2nd coming
>>>				of Christ
>>		3) its moral teachings are true
>>		4) when it speaks on science, history, or any other
>>			subject, it speaks correctly
>	B) since the Bible is God's Word, every person should submit to
>		its teachings as authoritative

Refuting Moral Relativism

1) <u>Moral Relativism</u>
    A) <u>Definition</u>
        1) no objective, universal moral values
        2) each person decides what is right for himself
    B) <u>Friedrich Nietzsche</u> (1844-1900) German philosopher
        1) if God is dead, then traditional values died with Him
        2) "soft values" of Christianity stifle human creativity
        3) Nietzsche recommended "hard values"
        4) supermen should create their own values through
           their will to power
        5) without God, there are no absolute moral values
    C) <u>Bertrand Russell</u> (1872-1970) British philosopher
        1) "outside human desires there is no moral standard."
        2) but what if a person desires to kill the innocent?
        3) Russell inconsistent (protested war, fought for gays)
    D) <u>A. J. Ayer</u> (1910-1989) British philosopher, moral commands
        merely express a person's subjective feelings
    E) <u>Jean-Paul Sartre</u> (1905-1980) French existentialist
        1) no objective meaning to life
        2) man must create his own values
    F) <u>Hedonism</u> (whatever brings pleasure is right, if it feels good
        do it, what about surgery to save a life?)
    G) <u>Utilitarianism</u> (the greatest good for the greatest number,
        who decides what the greatest good is?)
    H) <u>Situation Ethics</u> (Joseph Fletcher)
        1) ethics are relative to the situation
        2) love's decisions-made situationally, not prescribed
        3) Christian response:
           a) situation never determines what is right
           b) God determines what is right
           c) still, the situation often helps us determine which
             of God's laws should be applied
           d) when two of God's laws conflict (greater good)
             1) we must obey the greater good/higher law
             2) we receive an exemption from the lesser
                good/lower law
             3) absolute laws have no exceptions

2) <u>The Problem with Moral Relativism</u>
    A) when a person denies the absolute moral law . . .
        1) they cannot condemn the actions of another as evil
        2) without contradiction
        3) some type of absolute standard must be resurrected in
            order to make the value judgment
        4) if moral relativism is true, there is no basis from which
            to condemn the actions of Hitler
    B) television debate between a rabbi and a homosexual
    C) we all recognize actions as evil when we are wronged
    D) Christ's profound statement (Matthew 7:12)

3) <u>The Absolute Moral Law</u>
    A) <u>Definition</u>-"By a universal right is meant a duty that is
       binding on all men at all times and in all places."
       (*Introduction to Philosophy*, by Geisler and Feinberg)
    B) Bible declares much of God's absolute moral law-Ex 20; Mt 5
    C) God reveals many aspects of His absolute moral law in our
       consciences (Rm 2:14-15)

4) <u>The Moral Dilemma</u>
    A) does God will something because it is good?
       (then the moral law is above God)
    B) or, is something good merely because God wills it?
       (then moral law is arbitrary)
    C) Christian response:
        1) God wills something because it is good
           (the moral law is not arbitrary)
        2) it is good since it is consistent with God's good nature
           (the standard is not above God; God is the standard)
        3) God's will is subject only to His nature

5) <u>Argument for the Absolute Moral Law</u> (Rm 2:14-15)
    A) moral law doesn't originate with the individual, for then we
       could not call the actions of another person wrong (Hitler)
    B) isn't created by each society, for then we could not call the
       actions of another society wrong (Nazi Germany)
    C) doesn't come from a world consensus
        1) not infallible (flat world, geocentric universe)
        2) was slavery ever right?

3) world consensus, society only adds men quanitatively
4) we need a moral law qualitatively above man
5) if we condemn actions of the past, we need an eternal and unchanging moral law
D) a moral law qualitatively above all men
   1) it is not descriptive of the way things are
   2) it is prescriptive of the way things ought to be
   3) needs a moral lawgiver qualitatively above all men
   4) if we wish to condemn the actions of the past, this moral lawgiver must also be eternal and unchanging

The One True Faith

1) <u>The 7 World Views Examined</u>
   A) <u>Atheism</u> (the belief there is no God)
      1) arguments are invalid and self-refuting
      2) no adequate explanation for the existence of universe, personality, or morality
      3) theistic arguments disprove atheism
   B) <u>Pantheism</u> (God is the universe)
      1) fails to explain the existence of evil and the finite self
      2) reincarnation offers no reason to be moral or charitable
      3) if God is unknowable, how could we know that pantheism is true?
      4) if the world is an illusion, how can we be sure of anything?
      5) can we really live like evil is an illusion?
   C) <u>Panentheism</u> (the universe is God's body)
      1) God cannot be both finite and infinite in His basic nature
      2) a finite, changing God needs an infinite, non-changing God to ground its existence
   D) <u>Deism</u> (God created universe, but doesn't intervene)
      1) creation is God's greatest miracle
      2) therefore, He is able to perform lesser miracles
      3) it seems that He would also be willing to intervene
      4) laws of nature aren't prescriptive, they're descriptive
      5) God can supersede the laws of nature
   E) <u>Finite Godism</u> (God is limited because of evil)
      1) a finite god needs an infinite Cause
      2) a finite god doesn't deserve worship
      3) a finite god doesn't guarantee the defeat of evil
      4) evil does not prove that God cannot be all-powerful
         a) God will defeat evil in the future
         b) God has allowed evil for the purpose of a greater good (free will, courage, love enemies)
         c) this is the best possible way to achieve the best possible world
         d) no one fully understand God's ways (Isa 55:8-9)
         e) child in surgery questions father's motives

F) <u>Polytheism</u> (many gods)
    1) several gods would limit each other
    2) finite gods need an infinite Cause to ground their
       existence
    3) the infinite Cause would be God, not the lesser gods
    4) the identity of lesser gods (1 Cor 10:19-20)
H) <u>Theism</u> (the belief in one personal, infinite God who is both
    immanent and transcendant) Only this world view is
    supported by the evidence

2) <u>The 3 Main Theistic Religions (Judaism, Islam, Christianity)</u>
  A) <u>Judaism</u>
    1) Christ fulfilled their Old Testament prophecies
    2) devolved into salvation by human effort
    3) refuted through historical apologetics (Christ's Deity)
  B) <u>Islam</u>
    1) many contradictions in the Koran
    2) teaches salvation by human effort
    3) refuted through historical apologetics (Christ's deity)
  C) <u>Christianity</u>
    1) teaches salvation by God's grace (Eph 2:8-9;
      Mt 19:25-26)
    2) confirmed by historical apologetics
    3) superior to other theistic religions (God's justice,
      holiness, love, grace/Christ's substitutionary death)

Course Overview
Argument for Christianity as the One True Faith

1) there must be an eternal uncaused Cause of the universe

2) since the universe has design and morality, its Cause must be an intelligent and moral Designer

3) eyewitnesses recorded that Jesus rose from the dead and claimed to be God and Savior

4) these eyewitnesses were sincere-they were willing to die for their testimony

5) therefore, Jesus rose from the dead and claimed to be God and Savior

6) His resurrection proves He is God and Savior, and not a liar or a lunatic

7) Jesus called the Old Testament God's Word and promised to preserve His teachings (also God's Word) through the apostles

8) therefore, the Bible is God's Word

9) since the Bible is God's Word, its morality should be adhered to by all

10) since the Bible teaches salvation by God's grace alone through faith alone in Jesus alone, then all other belief systems are not salvific

AUGUSTINE (354-430AD)

1) Most famous works
   A) Confessions
   B) City of God
2) Conversion from Manicheanism (metaphysical dualism)
3) The problem of evil
   A) evil is a privation
   B) caused by abuse of human & angelic free will
   C) God allows evil for purpose of a greater good
4) Influenced by Plato's thought
   A) the invisible world of unchanging, eternal ideas or truths
   B) Augustine placed these ideas in the mind of God
   C) we cannot perceive the unchanging truths of things unless illuminated by God (Jn 1:9)
5) Argument for God's existence
   A) we have unchanging, eternal ideas in our minds
   B) but our minds are not the adequate cause for these unchanging, eternal ideas (our minds are changing & limited by time)
   C) only an unchanging, eternal Mind (God) is an adequate cause of the unchanging, eternal ideas
6) Refutation of Skepticism
   A) it is rationally inconsistent
      1) skeptics claim to suspend judgment on all things (man cannot know)
      2) however, skeptics do not suspend judgment on their skepticism (they claim to know that man cannot know)
   B) it cannot be consistently lived (even skeptics do not suspend judgment when it comes to eating, protecting oneself, etc.)
7) Time & Eternity
   A) no time before creation (Zeno's paradox)
   B) God exists in eternity (outside time)

8) Divine Sovereignty & Human Free Will
    A) before fall (able to not sin)
    B) after fall (not able to not sin)
    C) after conversion (able to not sin)
    D) after glorification (not able to sin)

ANSELM (1033-1109AD)

Two types of the Ontological Argument
    A) God is defined as the greatest conceivable Being
        1) God must exist
        2) for, if He did not exist, we could conceive of
            a greater Being (a Being with the same
            attributes but also exists)
        3) Kant's criticism (existence is not a predicate)
    B) God is defined as a Necessary Being
        1) a Necessary Being cannot not exist
        2) therefore, God must exist
        3) Geisler's criticism (it is logically possible that
            nothing exists)

THOMAS AQUINAS (1225-1274)

1) Most famous work - Summa Theologica
2) Influenced by Aristotle
    A) everything in the mind was first in the senses
        except the mind itself (blank slate)
    B) active mind & receptive mind
    C) act & potency
    D) essence & existence
    E) first principles of knowledge (self-evident)
        1) identity (being is being)
        2) noncontradiction (being is not nonbeing)
        3) excluded middle (either being or nonbeing)

       4) causality (nonbeing cannot cause being)

       5) finality (every being acts for an end)

   F) basic reliability of sense perception

   G) rejected ontological argument (Aquinas started with sense data)

   H) rejected kalaam cosmological argument

       1) Aristotle believed the universe was eternal

       2) Aquinas accepted Bible's account of creation

       3) Aquinas believed the beginning of the universe could not be proven through reason

3) Doctrines of Reason (natural revelation)

   A) could be proven through human reason

   B) 5 ways to prove God's existence

       1) from motion to an Unmoved Mover

       2) from effects to a First Cause

       3) from contingent beings to a Necessary Being

       4) from degrees of perfection to a Most Perfect Being

       5) from the guidance of mindless nature to the Intelligent Designer

   C) Can only be one infinitely perfect Being

   D) God is the cause of all perfections that exist

       1) therefore, He must have all these perfections

       2) He is an infinite Being

       3) He must have all these perfections to an infinite degree

   E) God talk

       1) not univocal (totally the same)

       2) not equivocal (totally different)

       3) not anological (similar)

       4) solution - univocal terms applied to God in an analogical way

       5) God is infinitely holy

       6) man is finitely holy

   F) Natural Law (God's eternal laws written in our hearts, Rm 2:14-15)

4) Doctrines of Faith (Supernatural Revelation)
  A) cannot be proven through reason
  B) supernatural revelation is needed
  C) the Trinity, the incarnation, etc.
  D) miracles (evidence for doctrines of faith)
5) Aquinas' View of Faith
  A) "belief that" (the intellect)
  B) "belief in" (the will)

BONAVENTURE (1221-1274)

1) Disagreed with Aquinas
2) Aquinas only used cosmological argument from
  existential causality
3) Bonaventure used the Kalaam Cosmological Argument
  A) the universe had a beginning
  B) everything that had a beginning needs a cause
  C) the universe needs a cause

RENE DESCARTES (1596-1650)

1) Methodological Skepticism
  A) doubted everything to find a point of certainty
  B) from this point of certainty all truth would be
    deduced
  C) "cogito urgo sum" (I think therefore I am)
2) He tried to prove everything with rational certainty
3) He left no room for Divine revelation
4) led to the enlightenment (rationalism, deism)
5) used ontological argument for God's existence
6) his system broke down (evil demon deceiving man)

BLAISE PASCAL (1623-1662)

1) Major Apologetic Work - Pensees
1) Opposed to Descartes' pure rationalism
2) Realized man is more than just a rational being
    A) "The heart has its reasons of which reason knows nothing"
    B) the heart = intuition, knowledge of first principles, the will, emotions
    C) pure rationalism leaves no room for revelation
4) Opposed to traditional arguments for God's existence
5) The paradox of man (he is both wretched & great)
6) The human condition (one way street to death)
7) Man's response to this hopeless condition
    A) diversion (dancing, sports, career, etc.)
    B) indifference (lack of interest in eternal things)
    C) self-deception (deny wretchedness & death, Jer 17:9)
8) Historical Evidences for Christianity
    A) fulfilled prophecies
    B) history & survival of the Jews
    C) miracles & resurrection of Christ
9) Pascal's Wager
    A) not an attempt to prove God's existence
    B) it is a plea for people to seek God & desire that He exists (those who seek God will find Him, Jer 29:13)
    C) The Choices
        1) If you wager on God
            a) if He exists, you win eternal life
            b) if He doesn't exist, you lose nothing
        2) If you wager against God
            a) if He does not exist, you win nothing
            b) if He does exist, you lose everything
    D) The wise man will wager that God exists
        1) he has nothing to lose & everything to gain
        2) therefore, he will wager his life on God

10) Pascal's assessment
-"there are only two classes of persons who can be called reasonable: those who serve God with all their heart because they know Him and those who seek Him with all their heart because they do not know Him."

LEIBNIZ (1646-1716)

1) used the ontological argument for God's existence
2) used the cosmological argument from sufficient reason for God's existence
   - A) there must be an explanation for everything that exists
   - B) the things that exist in the universe are explained by other things (we need air, food, water, parents, etc.)
   - C) adding all the things in the universe together will not give an explanation for the existence of the universe
   - D) there must exist some Being which contains in itself the explanation for its own existence (God is uncaused)
   - E) this self-explained Being is the explanation for all else that exists
   - F) otherwise, there is no explanation why anything exists at all

WILLIAM PALEY (1743-1805)

1) used the teleological argument for God's existence
2) Paley's Watchmaker argument

PHILOSOPHERS WHO ATTACKED TRADITIONAL APOLOGETICS

1) Immanuel Kant (1724-1804)
    A) we can know reality as it appears to us
    B) we cannot know reality as it is
    C) transcendental categories are necessary for human knowledge (similar to Platonic ideas)
    D) human reason, in order to function, accepts certain transcendental illusions as true, though they cannot be proven by reason (example - causality)
    E) antinomies or contradictions exist that cannot be reconciled through human reason
    D) we could not prove God through pure reason
    E) still, we must assume God's existence and life after death if we are to make sense of our sense of morality (practical reason, a moral argument for God's existence)

2) Hegel (1770-1831)
    A) the dialectical view of history
    B) thesis, antithesis, synthesis
    C) idea of absolute truth rejected

3) Soren Kierkegaard (1813-1855)
    A) the Father of Modern Existentialism
    B) subjective beliefs more important than objective truth
    C) overemphacized the will
    D) deemphacized the intellect
    E) religious faith is a blind leap of faith into the nonrational realm
    F) religious beliefs cannot be defended
    G) they can only be believed (fideism)

4) <u>David Hume (1711-1776)</u>
    A) denied the existence of innate ideas
    C) Hume was an empiricist (truth found only
        through 5 senses)
    B) Hume was a skeptic
    C) we cannot prove causality with certainty (rejects
        cosmological arguments)
    D) we can only know things with a high degree of
        probability
    E) Hume & miracles
        1) wise man only accepts the most probable
           option
        2) laws of nature have a high degree of
           probability
        3) miracles violate the laws of nature
        4) miracles are highly improbable
        5) the wise man will always reject miracles
    F) Hume & the teleological argument
        1) doesn't prove only one designer
        2) designer or designers could be evil
        3) designer or designers could be finite

5) <u>Friedrich Nietzsche (1844-1900)</u>
    A) proclaimed "God is dead"
    B) believed man created God through his primitive
        imagination & wishful thinking
    C) the human race has intellectually matured
    D) now, God is seen to be non-existent
    E) still, even atheist intellectuals were living
        inconsistently with their world view
    F) for if God is dead, then traditional moral values
        have died with Him
    G) Nietzsche redefined the good as "the will to
        power"
    H) He rejected the "soft values" of Christianity
    I) He recommended "hard values"

J) He called for a group of "supermen" to arise with the courage to create their own values

K) Nietzsche predicted the atheist of the twentieth century would realize the consequences of a world without God

L) without God there are no moral absolutes

M) man is free to play God & create his own values

N) Nietzsche predicted the twentieth century would therefore be the bloodiest century in the human history

O) Nietzsche died insane

P) Hitler and the Nazis turned to Nietzsche's works for the intellectual justification for their barbaric acts

Cornelius Van Til (1895-1987)

Apologetic Methodology: Transcendental Presuppositionalism

Apologetics Works: The Defense of the Faith (179-180; 298-299)
                          Christian Apologetics

1) rejected traditional apologetics

2) Calvinism - regeneration precedes faith

3) the Bible is self-authenticating

4) apologetics must start with the presupposition that the Triune God
   exists and has authoritatively revealed Himself in Scripture

5) all non-Christian reasoning presupposes human autonomy

6) all reasoning is circular (we argue from our conclusions, not to
   them)

7) the transcendental argument (the necessary conditions for human
   knowledge), all human thought and moral judgments would be
   impossible if Christianity is not true. "If God does not exist, we
   know nothing." "Self-consciousness presupposes God-
   consciousness." Arguing about the existence of air is similar to
   arguing about the existence of God. One needs air in order to
   argue.

8) all men know God exists, but they deceive themselves & suppress
   this truth (Rm 1:18-22)

9) no neutral ground (all are biased)

10) we do have common ground (we all live in God's universe; moral
    values, reason, etc.)

11) for argument's sake, Christians can place themselves within the unbeliever's presupposition to show that one has to presuppose the truth of Christianity just to raise an objection against Christianity. (Greg Bahnsen - "There's no way a person could get moral values or rationality from molecules in motion.")

12) God is above logic (above the law of non-contradiction)

13) inductive, probabilistic arguments for Christianity are unacceptable (transcendental argument - impossibility of the contrary)

14) we interpret facts by our presuppositions, not visa versa

15) God's thoughts & man's thoughts do not intersect at any point (all our knowledge of God is analogical)

16) only Christianity gives meaning to life, all other world views lead to irrationality & chaos

17) scientific induction makes no sense in a Godless universe (only the Christian God guarentees the uniformity of nature)

GORDON CLARK (1902-1985)

Apologetic Methodology: Dogmatic Presuppositionalism

Apologetic Works: Three Types of Religious Philosophy
Clark Speaks From the Grave
An Introduction to Christian Philosophy
Religion, Reason, and Revelation
A Christian View of Men and Things
Thales to Dewey (534)

1) rejected traditional apologetics (unaided human reason cannot arrive at truths about God)

2) rejected empiricism (rational conclusions cannot be drawn from sense experience alone, Clark also denied the basic reliability of sense perception & considered induction a fallacy)

3) rejected rationalism (reason cannot prove everything, it cannot prove its own first principles, something must be presupposed)

4) rejected irrationalism (if we allow contradictions, all thought and communication becomes meaningless)

5) unaided human reason results in skepticism (Hume, Kant, Hegel)

6) Clark's view is dogmaticism (we should dogmatically presuppose the existence of the Triune God & the truth of the Bible)

7) everyone must presuppose something

8) since rationalism & empiricism have failed to make life meaningful, we should presuppose the truth of Christianity

9) Clark's response to Kant - "God has fashioned both the mind and the world so that they harmonize." The innate ideas God has given us do correspond to reality. (without presupposing God, Kant's dilemma remains)

10) only Christianity is self-consistent and gives meaning to life & moral experience

11) only Christianity supports the existence of truth & the possibility of knowledge

12) used law of non-contradiction to refute non-Christian belief systems

13) God is logic, law of non-contradiction flows from His nature

14) Calvinism - regeneration precedes faith (we can't convince anyone of the truth of Christianity, regeneration by God is necessary)

15) problem of evil
   a) God predetermined what we will do (man is not free)
   b) God is the ultimate cause of sin (man is the author or immediate cause of sin)
   c) we are responsible to God for our sin
   d) there is no one above God to whom God is responsible

Francis Schaeffer (1912-1984)

Apologetic Methodology: Verificational Presuppositionalism

Apologetic Works: <u>The God Who is There</u>
<u>Escape From Reason</u>
<u>He is There and He is not Silent</u>

1) The line of despair (<u>Trilogy</u>, 8, 15, 16)
    A) modern man (post-modern man) has abandoned the idea of absolute truth
    B) Hegel (synthesis, rejected antithesis)
    C) Kierkegaard (synthesis could not be achieved through reason; leap of blind faith into non-rational realm needed)
    D) modern existentialism (life is absurd & meaningless, we must create meaning for ourselves - Sartre, optimism)
    E) nihilism (everything is meaningless & chaotic - despair)
    F) philosophy/art/music/general culture/theology (54)
    G) Aldous Huxley & Timothy Leary (LSD - leap of faith)

2) man's dilemma
    A) man is noble, man is cruel
    B) only Christianity offers an adequate explanation
    C) man was created in God's image, man morally fell

3) the mannishness of man
    A) personality & ability to verbalize places man above the animal kingdom
    B) since we are created in God's image, God can communicate propositionally to us
    C) only a personal God could produce personal man
    D) deny a personal God & one denies the nobility of man or one takes a leap of blind faith
    E) what is the purpose of man?
        1) modern man has no answer
        2) Christianity (through Christ our personal relationship with the personal God is restored)
    F) moral values make no sense in a world without absolutes
    G) apart from Christian presuppositions, mail fails to distinguish reality from unreality, man from animal, & right from wrong (Gordon Lewis)

H) finite, fallen man cannot find certain knowledge if he
autonomously begins with himself

    1) only in Scripture can finite man find certain
(though not exhaustive) knowledge

    2) we have no final answers in regard to truth,
morals, or epistemology without God's
revelation in the Bible

I) only Christianity offers an adequate explanation of the
universe & man(even the atheist must live in God's world

4) Schaeffer's method of apologetics

    A) verificational presuppositionalism (he allows his
presuppositions to be tested much like that of a scientific
hypothesis)

    B) tests for truth

        1) must be noncontradictory & explain phenomenon in
question

        2) we must be able to live consistently with our theory

    C) the possible answers

        1) everything came from nothing (this is absurd)

        2) everything had an impersonal start (the impersonal
plus time plus chance have produced personal man,
this goes against all experience)

        3) personality is an illusion (man cannot live consistent
with this view)

        4) everything had a personal start (this alone adequately
explains the mannishness of man)

    D) Schaeffer's method of evangelism

        1) when witnessing, start where the nonbeliever is &
bring his thought to its logical conclusion (despair,
or the folly of his leap)

        2) John Cage, existentialist musician (eating mushrooms)

        3) Hindu student (moral relativism, boiling water)

    E) the final apologetic

    "By this all men will know that you are my disciples, if
you have love for one another." (John 13:35)

Norman Geisler

Apologetic Methodology: Traditional Apologetics (Thomism)

Apologetic Works: <u>Christian Apologetics</u>
                         <u>Philosophy of Religion</u>
                         <u>When Skeptics Ask</u>

* Geisler is one of the few traditional apologists who has taken some of the presuppositional objections to heart (he has not abandoned traditional apologetics; he has fine-tuned it)

1) methodology (how do we find truth?)
    A) agnosticism fails ("man cannot know" is a claim to know)
    B) pure rationalism fails (only proves what is false, reason cannot prove first principles)
    C) fideism fails (doesn't even test truth claims - it just believes, must assume law of non-contradiction to deny it)
    D) experientialism fails (no experience is self-interpreting, conflicting truth claims based on experience cannot be tested)
    E) evidentialism fails (facts don't come with built-in interpretations, we interpret facts by our world views & not the other way around)
    F) pragmatism fails (all truth must ultimately work but not everything that works is necessarily true, often lies work, we can't always see the long range results)
    G) combinationalism fails (adding leaky buckets will still not hold water, adding inadequate solutions does not give us an adequate solution)
    H) adequate tests for truth
        1) unaffirmability (test for falsity of world views)
        2) actual undeniability (test for truth of world views)
        3) systematic coherence (combinationalism - test for truth statements within a world view)
            a) consistency (must be non-contradictory)
            b) empirical adequacy (must explain all the relevant facts)
            c) experiential relevance (must be liveable)

2) theistic apologetics (what is the true world view?)
    A) deism fails (if God created the world, He is both able & willing to intervene in the world)

B) pantheism fails (fails to explain the existence of the finite
    self & the existence of evil, if God is unknowable how
    could we know pantheism is true?)
C) panentheism fails (a finite, changing god needs an infinite,
    non-changing God to ground its existence)
D) atheism fails (arguments are invalid & self-refuting, no
    explanation for the existence of the universe, personality,
    & morality)
E) theism is actually undeniable (C. A. - 238-239)

3) Christian apologetics (which theistic religion is true?)
    A) Islam & Judaism fail the test of systematic coherence
    B) Christianity passes the test of systematic coherence
        1) naturalism & supernaturalism (if God exists, miracles
          are possible)
        2) objectivism & history (history is objective as modern
          science, both deal with probabilities, miracle claims
          must be historically tested)
        3) historical reliability of the New Testament
        4) deity & authority of Jesus Christ
        5) inspiration & authority of the Bible

Title: Testing World Views
Speaker: Dr. Phil Fernandes, Institute of Biblical Defense
         P. O. Box 3264 * Bremerton, WA. 98310
         (360) 698-7382

Testing World Views

1) logical consistency—is the world view without contradictions in its essential points?

2) explanatory power—does the world view adequately explain the data of reality?

3) livability—can you live consistently with your world view?

4) existential power
    A) does it provide a sense of meaning in life?
    B) does it make sense of our moral & rational experience?
    C) does it meet our emotional & societal needs?

5) societal impact—does it enhance freedom, order, & human rights?

Examples of World Views

1) Christian Theism

2) Atheism

3) Skepticism

4) Pantheism
    A) other-worldly
    B) this-worldly

Truth, Morality, Miracles, & Evil

1) Truth
    A) "there is no absolute truth" (self-refuting)
    B) "we cannot know truth" (self-refuting)
    C) conclusion—there is absolute truth & we can know it

2) Morality
    A) "it is wrong to call others' actions wrong"
        (self-refuting)
    B) we all consider actions wrong when we are wronged
    C) absolute moral law above all individuals, societies,
        & any world consensus (absolute moral Lawgiver)

3) Miracles
    A) "natural laws prove that miracles are impossible"
    B) natural laws are descriptive, not prescriptive
    C) God created natural laws & can superceed or
        interrupt them whenever He so chooses
    D) God uses miracles to catch our attention &
        communicate to us (Bible, resurrection, etc.)

4) Evil
    A) "God cannot co-exist with evil & innocent human
        suffering"
    B) God did not create evil; He created the possibility for
        evil (free will)
    C) God did not force His love & will on us
    D) God allows evil for the purposes of a greater good
        —draw people to Himself, courage, love enemies
    E) evil is a corruption of something good (evil proves
        God's existence)
    F) God's ways & thoughts are far above human
        understanding (Isaiah 55:8-9)

Evidence for God's Existence

1) Some Traditional Arguments for God's Existence

A) <u>Cosomological Argument</u>—the universe had a beginning & therefore needs a cause (the first cause must be eternal).

B) <u>Moral Argument</u>—eternal, unchanging moral law that is above man implies an eternal, unchanging moral Lawgiver above man.

C) <u>Teleological Argument</u>—the design and order in the universe shows that the universe needs an intelligent designer

D) <u>Religious Experience</u>—all men sense a need for God.

E) <u>Absurdity of life without God</u>—if God does not exist, then life is without meaning, morality is not ultimately real, there is no life after death (punishments/rewards), no ultimate defeat of evil.

F) <u>Eternal, Unchanging Ideas</u>—cannot come from temporal, changing minds. There must be an eternal unchanging mind.

2) The Cumulative Case for God

A) Christian Theism is treated as a hypothesis

B) it is more reasonable to believe in God than to be an atheist

C) theism offers a more adequate explanation than atheism does for the following aspects of reality:

1) the beginning of the universe
2) the continued existence of the universe
3) the design & order in the universe
4) the possibility of human knowledge (human reason)
5) the existence of universal, eternal, unchanging truths (laws of logic)
6) the reality of universal, eternal, unchanging moral values (torturing innocent babies is wrong)
7) the meaning of life (purpose)
8) a reason to be optimistic about the future (hope)
9) a guarantee that evil will ultimately be defeated
10) feelings of guilt
11) fear of death
12) respect for human life

D) mere molecules in motion, combined with time and chance, cannot explain any of these factors

Common Arguments for God's Existence

1) the <u>ontological argument</u> (Anselm, Descartes)
    A) argues for God's existence from reason alone
    B) two types (Anselm)
        1) the greatest conceivable Being must have all
           perfections; existence is a perfection
        2) a Necessary Being, by definition, is a being
           that cannot not exist

2) the <u>teleological argument</u> (Paley, Aquinas)
    —the design & order in the universe show that the
       universe needs an intelligent Designer

3) <u>the moral argument</u> (Kant, Lewis)
    —eternal, unchanging moral laws that are above all
       mankind imply the existence of an eternal,
       unchanging moral Lawgiver

4) <u>the cosmological argument</u>
    A) <u>Aquinas (existential causality)</u>
        1) the totality of the universe is dependent
        2) it needs a Cause for its continuing existence
    B) <u>Bonaventure (kalam)</u>
        1) the universe had a beginning
        2) the beginning of the universe needs a Cause
    C) <u>Leibniz (sufficient reason)</u>
        1) everything that exists needs an explanation as
           to why it exists
        2) eventually we must arrive at a self-explained
           Being (explains its own existence)

World Religions

the non-Christian world religions reject Jesus, the biblical doctrine of salvation, & the doctrine of the Trinity

Judaism & Islam
- A) accepts existence of personal God
- B) rejects salvation through Christ & Christ's deity
- C) teaches salvation through works

Hinduism
- A) teaches that God is the impersonal universe (pantheism)
- B) teaches that man is God
- C) teaches reincarnation

Buddhism
- A) teaches atheism or pantheism
- B) teaches reincarnation

The New Age Movement

1) Definition of the New Age Movement
    A) current revival of ancient occultism (secret arts—Dt 29:29)
    B) immersing of the United States with Hindu/Eastern thought
    C) man is evolving towards a new age of peace & enlightenment

2) History of the New Age Movement
    A) has its roots in ancient occultism
    B) Theosophical Society—Helena Blavatsky—1875
    C) spiritual history of America
        —Christian theism/atheism/pantheism

3) New Age Influence (public schools, business, politics, science, UN, liberal Christianity, movies, psychology)

4) Common New Age Practices (astrology, ESP, eastern meditation, occultic healing, vegetarianism, wicca, fortunetelling, animal rights, ecological activism, channeling, visualization, astral travel, numerology, ect.)

5) Common New Age Beliefs
    A) pantheism (God is the universe; God is impersonal)
    B) self-deification (man is god)
    C) reincarnation (the soul passes through the cycle of death & rebirth; the soul is incarnated in many different bodies)
    D) illusionism (the world is an illusion)
    E) relativism
        1) no absolute truth
        2) no absolute moral laws
    F) evolution (the world & mankind are evolving)
    G) globalism (the coming one-world government)
    H) syncretism/religious pluralism (all religions will unite)
    I) new age (coming age of global peace & enlightenment)
    J) channeling (voluntary possession to allow spirit entities to speak through you)
    K) eastern meditation (emptying of mind; attempts to unite with God; opens mind to demonic influence)
    L) UFO movement (possible demonic deception)
    M) denial of essential Christian beliefs
        1) Jesus is one of several manifestations of God
        2) Jesus isn't the Savior; He didn't die for our sins
        3) man is already saved; man is God
        4) sin & hell are illusions
        6) denial of the Trinity; Christ's deity, & resurrection

Postmodernism

1) History of Western Culture
    A) Premodernism
        1) from ancient Greece through Medieval times
        2) widely believed assumptions:
            a) truth is absolute
            b) truth corresponds to reality
            c) human reason able to find truth
            d) universe made sense
            e) a reality beyond the 5 senses
        3) the Christian world view fit nicely into the premodern
           mindset & confirmed it
            a) infinite rational God created man in His image &
                the universe in an orderly way
            b) man could find truth in the universe
    B) Modernism
        1) Rene Descartes (1596-1650)
            a) tried to prove everything through reason alone
            b) "I think therefore I am"
        2) modernism = the attempt to find all truth with
           certainty through unaided human reason
        3) revelation from God—no longer needed
    C) Postmodernism (a reaction against modernism)
        1) modernism failed to find absolute truth & solve man's
           problems
        2) postmodernism rejects absolute truth & human
           reason's ability to find truth

2) Postmodern Views
    A) denies absolute truth (no metanarrative)
        —truth is relative to one's community or social group
    B) focuses on meaning, feelings, will
    C) focuses on community (not individual relativists,
        but cultural relativists)
    D) focuses on mystery, beauty, narratives
    E) denies absolute morality
    F) heavy emphasis on tolerance
    G) reject dichotomist thinking (either/or; true/false;
        right/wrong)
    H) reduce all authority to power
        1) authority = the right to be obeyed or believed
        2) power = the ability to make others obey or believe
    I) power narratives instead of rational arguments
    J) we create our own reality through language

K) deconstruction—replace author or speaker's meaning with meaning from our community (Black Christology, Liberation Theology, Gay Theology)

L) political correctness (can't tolerate any non-postmodernists)

3) <u>Refutation of Postmodernism</u>
   A) it is self-refuting
      1) "there is no absolute truth"
      2) "it is wrong to call any action wrong"
      3) reject moral absolutes while creating new moral absolutes
      4) even their language does not touch reality
      5) if every community has their own narrative & there is no metanarrative, then they cannot escape their community's narrative to critique the narrative of another community
      6) while condemning the metanarrative, postmodernism has become a metanarrative
      7) they divide all people into two groups
         a) those who accept dichotomies & those who don't
         b) they don't accept dichotomies
         c) but they are themselves dichotomists (point a)
   B) fails to give us any reason to be postmodern
   C) while proclaiming tolerance, they cannot tolerate any non-postmodernists
      1) once reason is abandoned, all that's left is shouting
      2) postmodernism is a vehicle for angry people who hate tradition to attain positions of power to overturn tradition

4) <u>The Christian Response to Postmodernism</u> (see handout)

Modernism

—all truth found through reason alone
—no need for revelation from God
—focuses on autonomous individual
—focuses on rational principles

we need to:
—emphasize the rational/explanatory power
   of the gospel (the Christian world view)
—appeal primarily to the mind

Postmodernism

—denies absolute truth
—focuses on meaning, feelings, will
—focuses on community
—focuses on mystery, beauty

we need to:
—emphasize the beauty of
   the redemption story
—appeal to the heart, emotions, & will

Hebrew   John 4:24   Greek   Modernism

spirit &
truth

Old   New   reason
Testament   Testament   elevated

Postmodernism

no
metanarrative

we may need to change our method,
but we can never change the message
(Hebrews 13:8; Jude 3)

The Jesus Seminar

1) What it is

A) group of New Testament scholars
B) began to meet in 1985, receives much media coverage
C) John Dominic Crossan, Robert Funk, Marcus Borg
D) originally 200 members, now about 74
E) voted on which sayings of Jesus were authentic
F) considered "Gospel of Thomas" on same level as 4 Gospels
G) color-coded "The Five Gospels" (1993)
    1) red = Jesus definitely said it
    2) pink = Jesus probably said it
    3) gray = Jesus possibly said it
    4) black = Jesus definitely did not say it

2) What's wrong with it

A) Gospel of John—no red, one pink, only a few gray
B) over 82% of Jesus' sayings in 4 Gospels are rejected
C) only 15 sayings of Jesus are red-lettered
D) supposedly, Jesus never claimed to be God, Messiah, or Savior
E) its members are a very small, radical subset of NT scholarship
F) almost half of the 74 members earned their graduate degrees from
    Harvard, Claremont, or Vanderbilt (extremely liberal)
G) European scholars are not represented
H) Evangelical scholars are not represented
I) 40 of the 74 members are relative unknowns
J) a bias against the supernatural
K) assume the Gospels are false until proven true
L) believe in a nonsupernatural original manuscript which no one has
    ever seen (usually called "Q")
M) Gospel of Thomas is a highly suspect gnostic document (140AD)
N) evidence for the reliability of the 4 Gospels is overwhelming:
    1) manuscript evidence   5) ancient creeds
    2) apostolic fathers   6) evidence for Christ's deity
    3) ancient secular authors   7) evidence for resurrection
    4) archaeological confirmation   8) additional evidence

Institute of Biblical Defense

P. O. Box 3264 * Bremerton, WA. 98310 * (360) 698-7382
www.biblicaldefense.org   Dr. Phil Fernandes, President

Mormonism

1) <u>History</u>
    A) founded by Joseph Smith in the 1820's
    B) Brigham Young became prophet & leader after Smith's death
    C) Wilford Woodruff—put a stop to polygamy
    D) 1978—Blacks allowed in Mormon priesthood

2) <u>Statistics</u>
    A) over 9 million Mormons worldwide
    B) headquarters—Salt Lake City, Utah

3) <u>Sacred Writings</u>—the Bible, the Book of Mormon, the Doctrine and Covenants, the Pearl of Great Price, the Journal of Discourses (prophecies of their living prophets)

4) <u>Inaccuracies in Mormon Scriptures</u> (Gleason Archer, Jr.)

5) <u>Mormon Heretical Theology</u>
    A) denial of the Trinity (they teach that the father, Son, & Holy Spirit are 3 separate gods)
    B) polytheism—belief in many gods (Isaiah 43:10)
    C) eternal progression (Mormon males can become gods) Genesis 3:1-7
    D) Jesus (spirit brother of Lucifer; still progressing in godhood; had several wives) Hebrews 13:8; John 1:1
    E) Bible (not the final Word of God-they add more sacred books) Jude 3; Ephesians 2:20; Hebrews 1:1-3; Proverbs 30:5-6
    F) salvation (salvation by faith in the Mormon Jesus, Mormon baptism, good works, & obedience to Mormon ordinances) Ephesians 2:8-9; John 3:16-18; 14:6; Matthew 19:25-26
    G) pre-existent spirit beings (before our conception)
    H) denial of the virgin birth (God the Father has a body)
    I) Mormon priesthood & temple services (Colossians 2:16-17)
    J) baptism for the dead/occultic temple rituals/genealogies
    K) polygamy (no longer practiced) Matthew 19:3-9
    L) three heavens (celestial, terrestrial, telestial)
    M) Mormon hell (only Satan, demons, & apostacized Mormons)

Institute of Biblical Defense

P. O. Box 3264 * Bremerton, WA. 98310 * (360) 698-7382
www.biblicaldefense.org   Dr. Phil Fernandes, President

Jehovah's Witnesses
The Watchtower Bible & Tract Society

1) <u>History</u>
    A) started by Charles Taze Russell (Pastor Russell) in 1870's
    B) Judge Rutherford suceeded Russell as president in 1917
    C) Nathan Homer Knorr became president in 1942 (NWT)
    D) Frederick W. Franz became president in 1977

2) <u>Statistics</u> (headquarters—Brooklyn, New York)
    —over 4 million members worldwide

3) <u>Heretical Theology</u>
    A) denial of Christ's deity (Jesus is a lesser god)
        1) Titus 2:13; John 1:1; 2 Peter 1:1; Colossians 2:9
        2) Jeremiah 23:5-6; Zechariah 14:5; Isaiah 9:6
    B) denial of the Trinity
        1) only the Father is God; Holy Spirit is just God's power
        2) Matthew 3:16-17; John 14:16, 26; 15:26; 16:7-11
    C) denial of the Holy Spirit's personality
        —Ephesians 4:30; Acts 8:29; 10:19; 13:2; 21:11
    D) denial of Christ's bodily resurrection
        —John 2:19-21; 20:26-27; Luke 24:36-43
    E) denial of salvation by grace & the atonement
        —Romans 3:10, 20-23; Ephesians 2:8-9; 1 Peter 3:18;
        2 Corinthians 5:15, 21
    F) denial of Christ's visible return
        A) Jesus invisibly returned to Brooklyn, NY in 1914
        B) Revelation 1:7; Matthew 24:23-31; Acts 1:9-12
    G) denial of the human soul (soul-sleep)
        —Philippians 1:21-24; Lk 16:19-31; 2 Corinthians 5:8
    H) denial of eternal torment (annihilation)
        —Revelation 14:9-11; 20:10, 15; Mark 9:47-48
    I) disrespect for human government
        —Romans 13:1-7; Mark 12:17
    J) misunderstanding concerning God's name (Jehovah)
        A) YHWH = Jehovah (Jesus is called Jehovah in OT)
        B) Matthew 6:9 (Jesus told us to call God "Father")
    K) failed prophecies
        —Deuteronomy 18:20-22; Matthew 7:15-23; 24:23-27
    L) their Bible is a perversion of God's Word (John 1:1; 8:58)

Refuting the Cults

1) <u>Paul's warning about false teachers (2 Cor 11; Gal 1:8-9)</u>
    A) they proclaim another Jesus & another Gospel
    B) they are inspired by a different spirit (not the Holy Spirit)

2) <u>Christ's warning about false prophets (Mt 7:15-23)</u>

3) <u>Mormonism/Latter-Day Saints</u>
    A) Jesus is one of many gods, He is progressing in godhood
    B) Mormon men can become gods
    C) salvation through belief in the Mormon Jesus, good works,
        and obedience to the Mormon ordinances

4) <u>Jehovah's Witnesses</u>
    A) Jesus is a lesser god, He is Michael the Archangel become a
        man, He was God's first creation
    B) salvation through believing in the JW Jesus and obeying
        God's commands
    C) soul-sleep & annihilation of the wicked

5) <u>New Age Movement</u>
    A) God is the universe (Pantheism)
    B) Jesus is one of many manifestations of God
    C) Jesus exercised His God-consciousness better than most
        people have
    D) salvation through recognizing we are God & reincarnation

6) <u>Unitarian Universalists</u>
    A) Jesus is not God
    B) He is a mere man, didn't exist before conception
    C) everyone will be saved, man is not fallen

7) <u>the true Jesus of the Bible</u>
    A) the kenosis (Php 2:5-8)
        —Jesus veiled His glory and voluntarily chose not to use
            certain divine attributes while on earth
    B) the hypostatic union (Jn 1:1, 14; Col 2:9; 1 Tm 2:5)
        1) Jesus is one person with two distinct natures forever
        2) Jesus is fully God & fully man (He is not merely man)
        3) Jesus always existed as God the 2nd Person of the
            Trinity, but He added a human nature at a point in
            time (2,000 years ago)

8) <u>the true teaching on salvation</u>
    A) salvation is by God's grace alone through faith alone in
        the true Jesus alone (Eph 2:8-10; Jn 3:16-18; 14:6)
    B) Christians don't do good works to get saved, they do good
        works because they are saved (Rm 3:10, 23, 31)
    C) good works are not the cause of salvation, they are the
        result of salvation (Jm 2:26)

Institute of Biblical Defense

P. O. Box 3264 * Bremerton, WA. 98310 * (360) 698-7382
Dr. Phil Fernandes, President * www.biblicaldefense.org

Evidence for Jesus' Resurrection

1) James' changed life
2) Paul's changed life
3) Peter's changed life
4) the empty tomb
5) women were the first witnesses
6) Joseph of Arimathea's tomb
7) apostles died martyr's deaths
8) apostles believed they saw Jesus alive numerous times
      (1 Corinthians 15:3-8)
9) resurrection preached in Jerusalem (Acts 1-12)
10) worship day changed to Sunday
11) the church grew rapidly in Jerusalem
12) the Shroud of Turin?

Evidence for Christ's Deity

1) Jesus called God "Abba"
2) Jesus' "truly, truly" statements
3) Jesus' favorite title for Himself was "Son of Man"
4) Jesus was considered an exorcist by friend & foe
5) Jesus claimed to be able to forgive sin
6) Jesus believed He had authority over the temple
7) Jesus believed He could perform miracles
8) Jesus believed He would usher in the Kingdom of God
9) Jesus believed a person's eternal destiny rested on Him
10) Jesus fulfilled numerous Old Testament prophecies

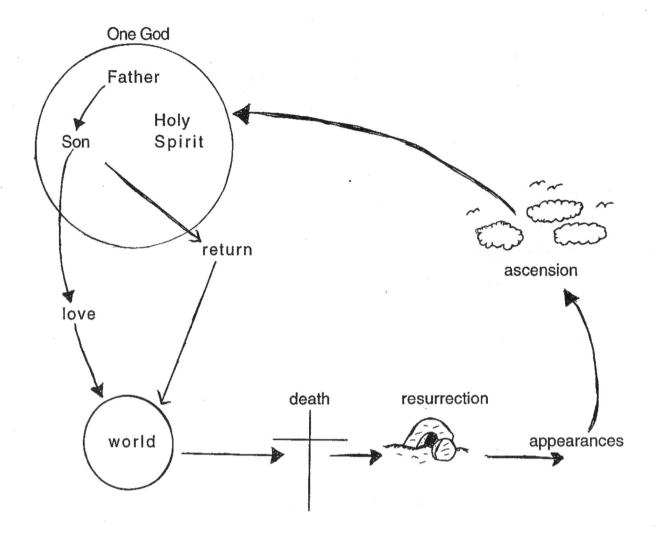

10 Gospel Truths

1) only one God
2) God is 3 Persons
3) God the Father loves the world
4) God the Father sent His Son into the world
5) God's Son became a man
6) He died on the cross for our sins
7) He rose from the dead on the third day
8) He appeared to His disciples
9) He ascended to heaven
10) He will return someday

Our Threefold Response

1) admit we are sinners & we cannot save ourselves
2) trust in Jesus alone for salvation
3) trust in Jesus & His Word for daily living

Dr. Phil Fernandes

About the Founder

The Institute of Biblical Defense was founded by Phil Fernandes in 1990 to aid Christians in their defense of the gospel. Fernandes has earned the following degrees: a Ph.D. in Philosophy of Religion from Greenwich University, a Doctor of Ministry and a Master of Biblical Studies from Bethany Theological Seminary, a Master of Arts in Religion from Liberty University, and a Bachelor of Theology from Faraston Theological Seminary. He has lectured on Creation Science and debated opponents of Christianity in the public schools and on college campuses. He is the Pastor of Trinity Bible Fellowship in Bremerton, WA. and the Professor of Theology and Apologetics at the Faraston Theological Seminary Bremerton Extension. Fernandes is a member of the following professional societies: the Evangelical Theological Society, the Evangelical Philosophical Society, and the Society of Christian Philosophers. Due to his extensive knowledge of Christian thought, Fernandes has been a frequent guest on television and radio talk shows. Fernandes and his lovely wife Cathy reside in Bremerton, WA. They are the proud parents of their daughter Melissa, who is married to Tim Smith.

Made in United States
Troutdale, OR
05/31/2024